emotional rescue

STUDIO PRESS BOOKS

First published in the UK in 2018 by Studio Press Books,
an imprint of Kings Road Publishing, part of Bonnier Books UK,
The Plaza, 535 King's Road, London, SW10 0SZ

www.studiopressbooks.co.uk
www.bonnierbooks.co.uk

Printed Under License ©2018 Emotional Rescue
www.emotional-rescue.com

3 5 7 9 10 8 6 4

ISBN 978-1-78741-318-4

Printed in Turkey

The Wit & Wisdom of
GRANDMA

STUDIO PRESS

Thanks to their Grandma, they learned at an early age how to save money! (They used hers instead!)

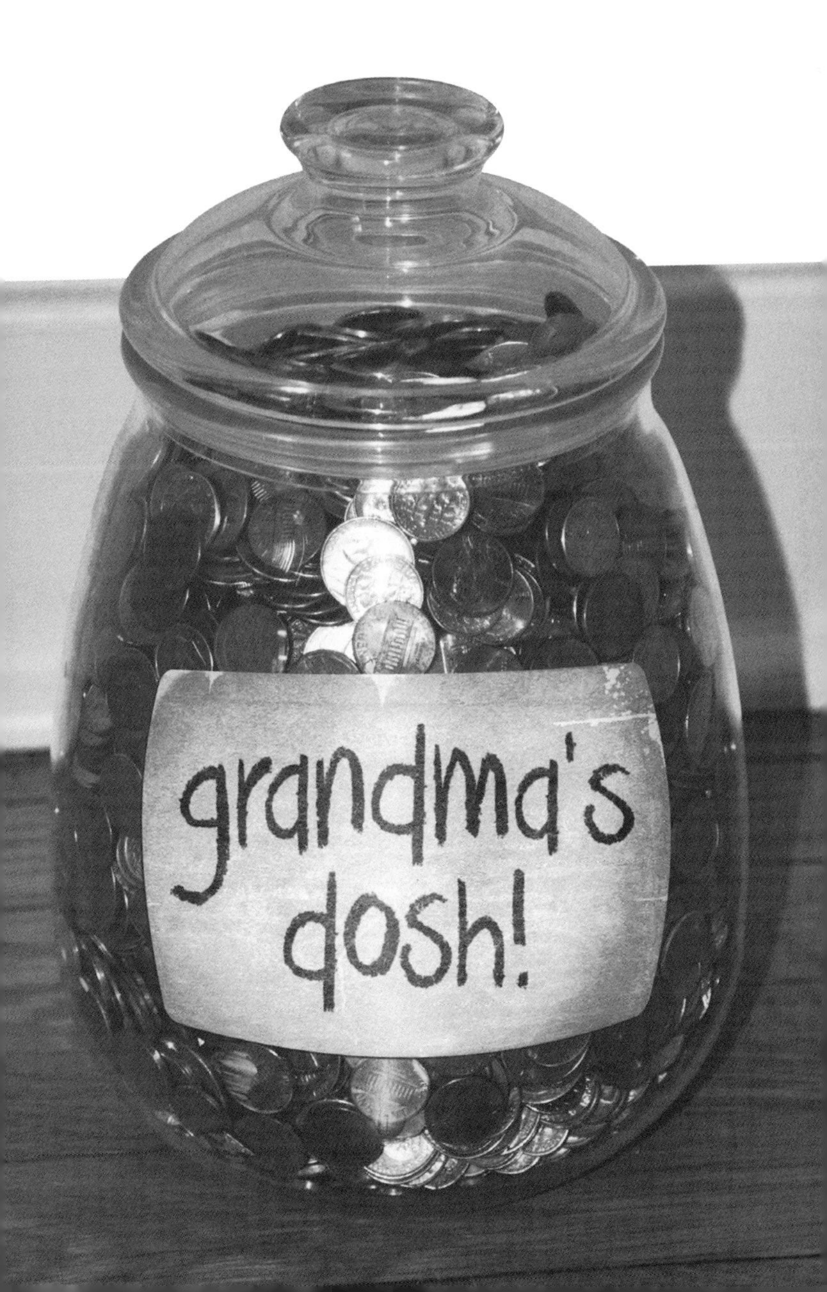
grandma's
dosh!

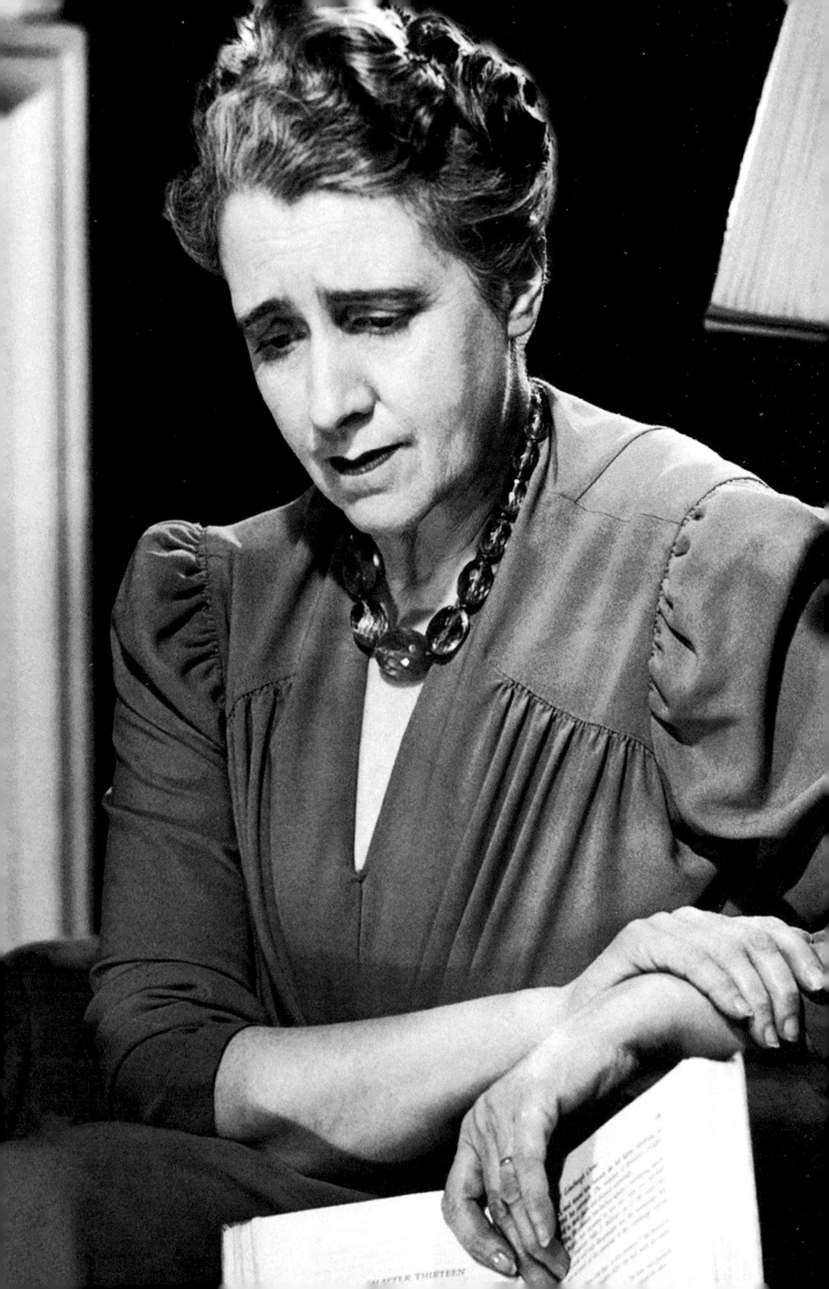

Grandma frequently needed to consult the owner's manual to find out how to operate her teenage grandkids.

As far as Grandma was concered, chocolate was healthy and she could prove it.
1) Chocolate come from cocoa.
2) Cocoa comes from a plant.
3) That makes chocolate a salad!

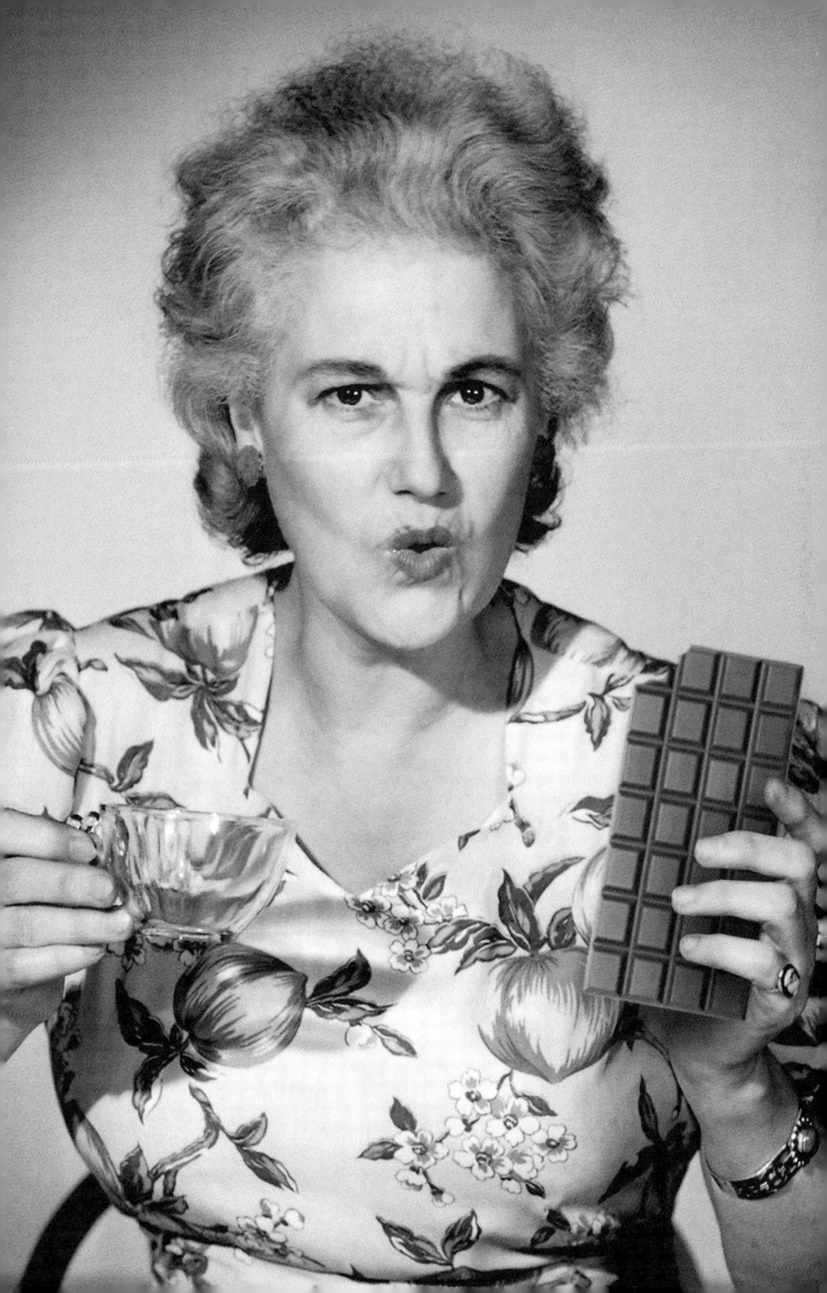

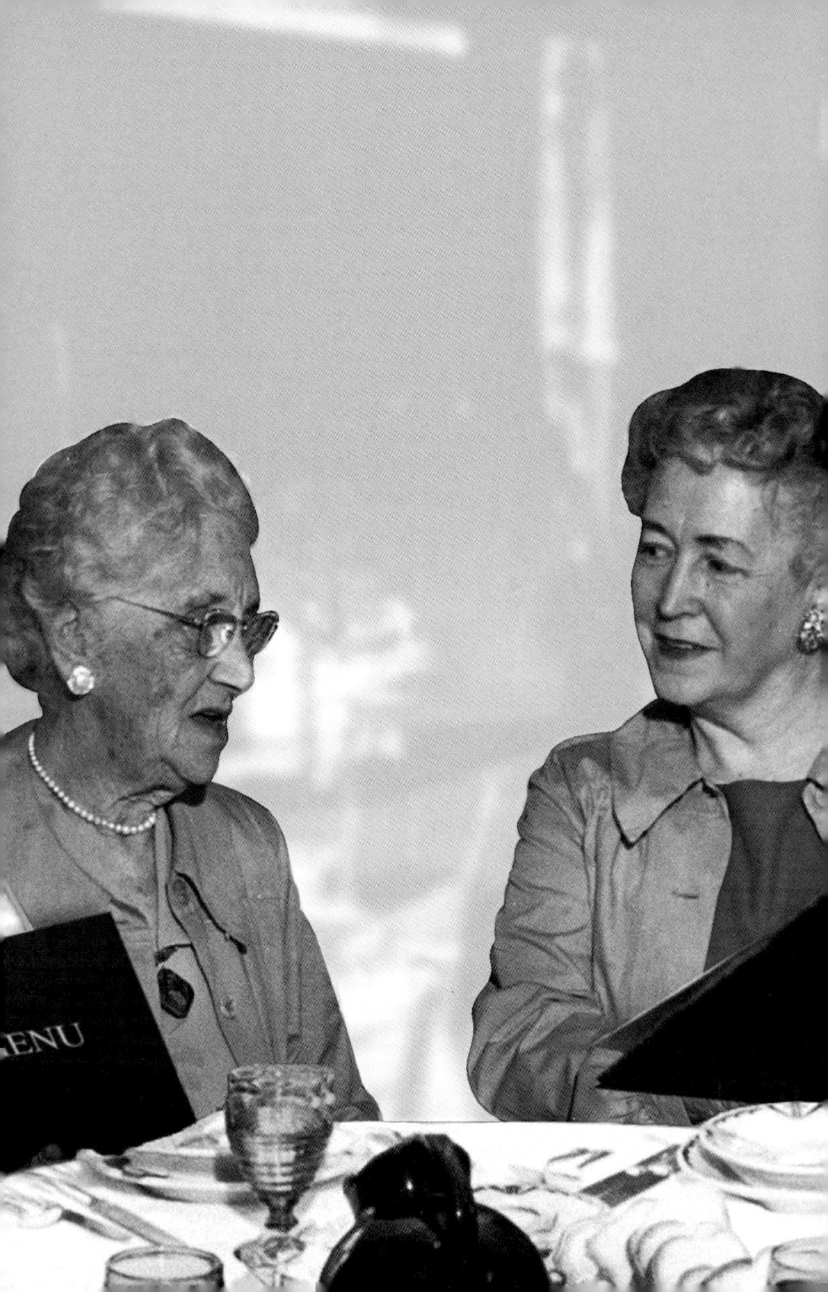

"ooo, I'm really in the mood for a Quickie!" said Grandma. "It's pronounced 'Quiche'!" replied her friend.

Grandma found that the most time-consuming part of online shopping was scrolling down to the year of her birth.

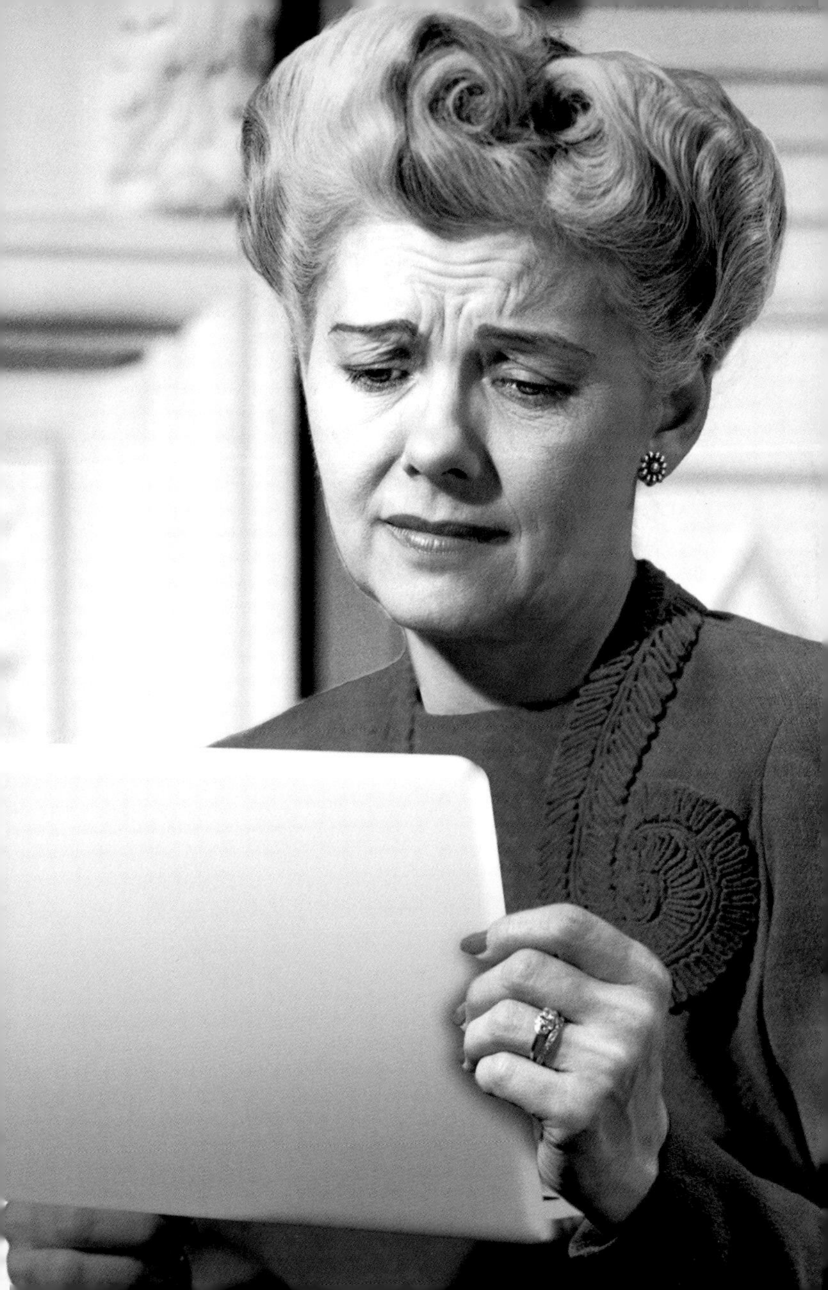

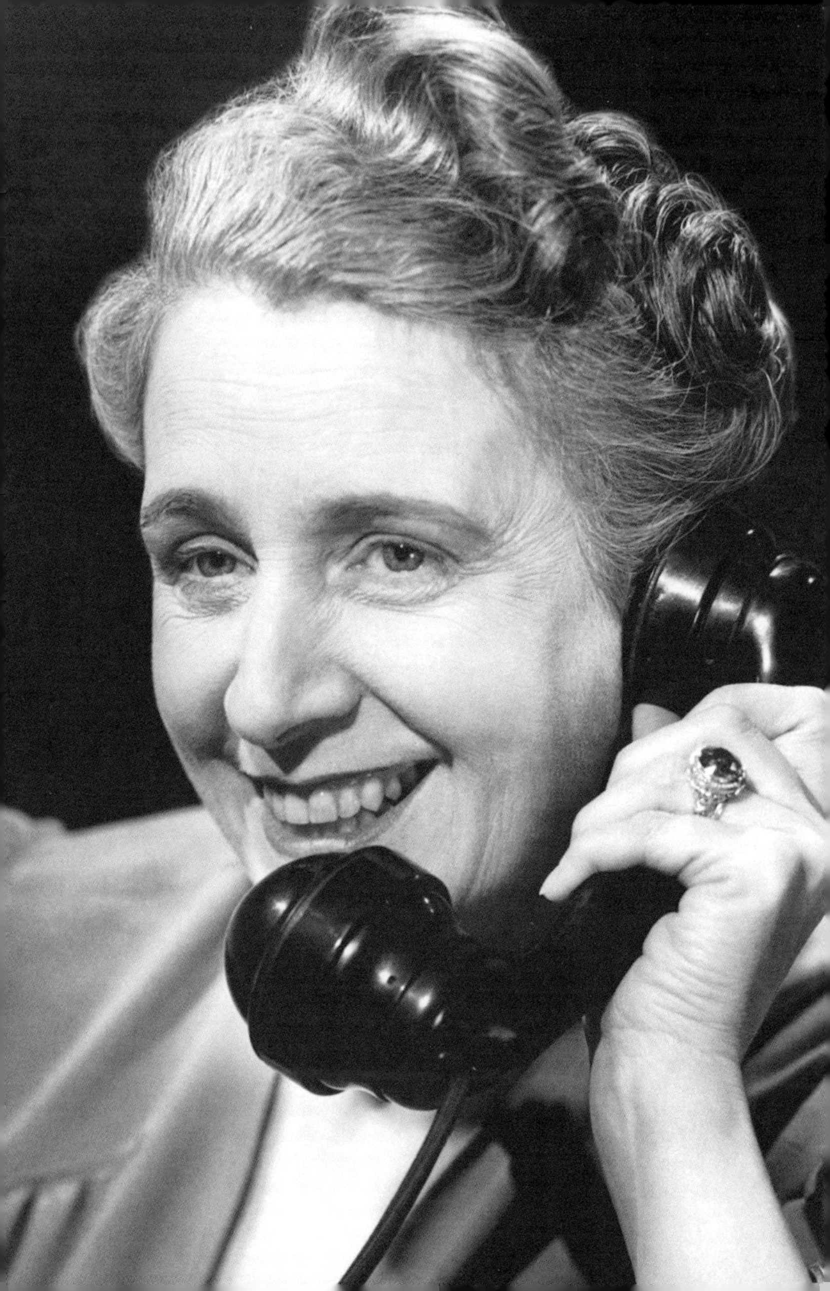

It was clear that Grandma's phone needed updating!

Sometimes when Grandma laughed, the tears would run down her legs!

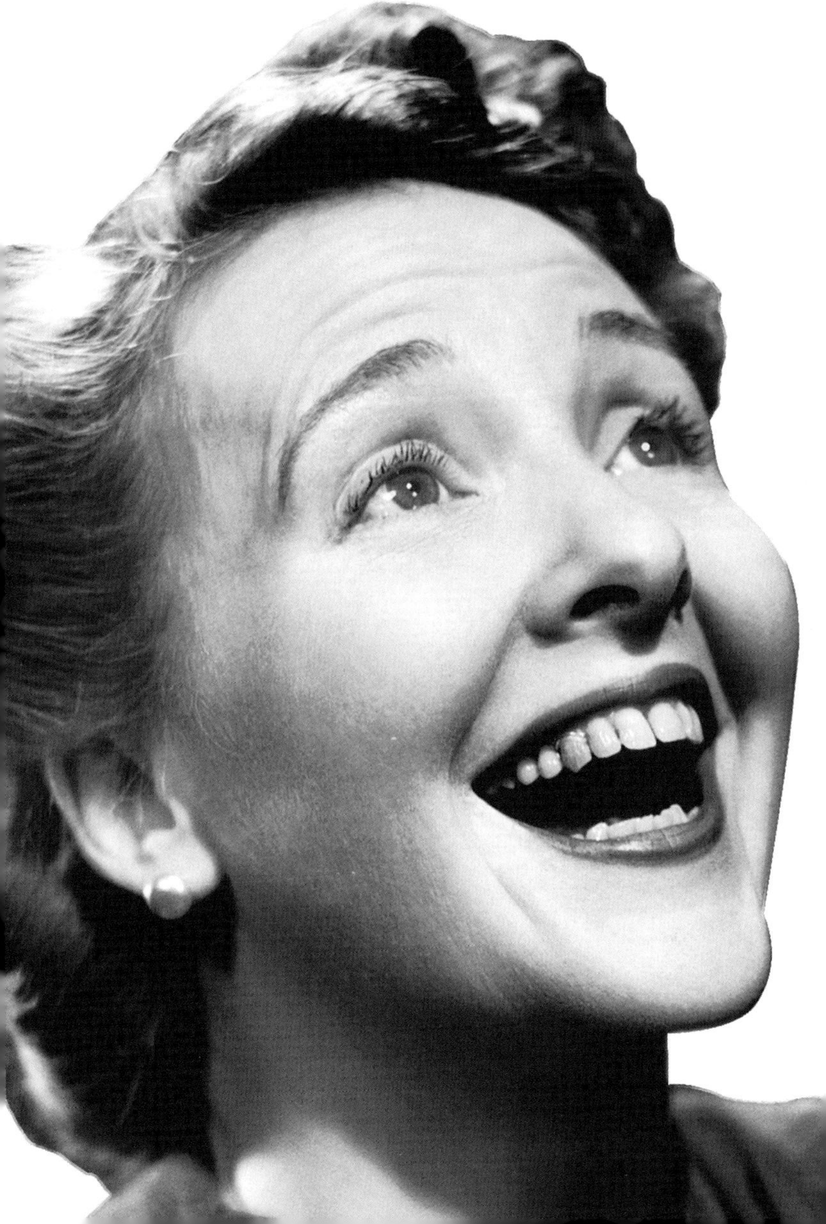

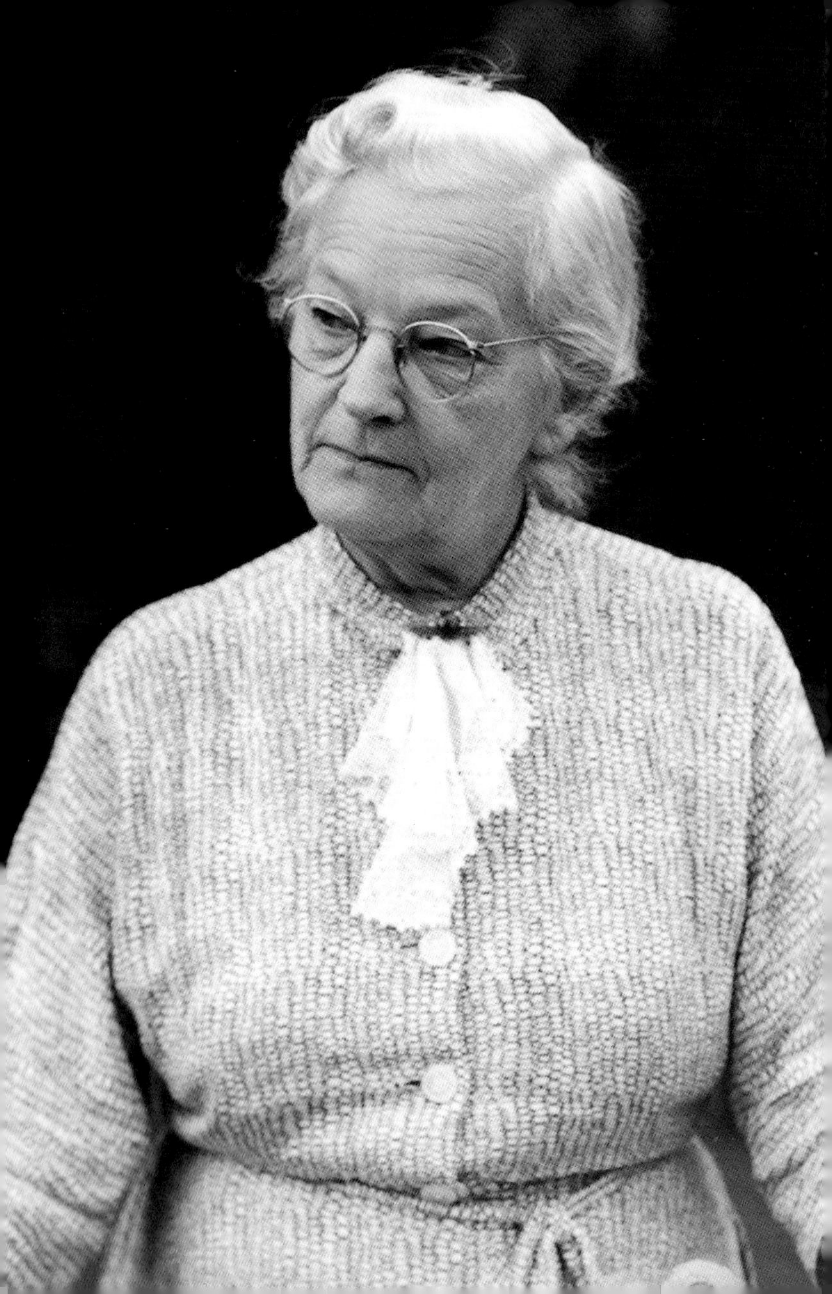

Grandma referred to her age
as the 'wonder years'.
She'd frequently walk into a room
and wonder why she was there.

"So," asked Grandma,
"What do we do if we get trumps?"
"Usually, I open a window!"

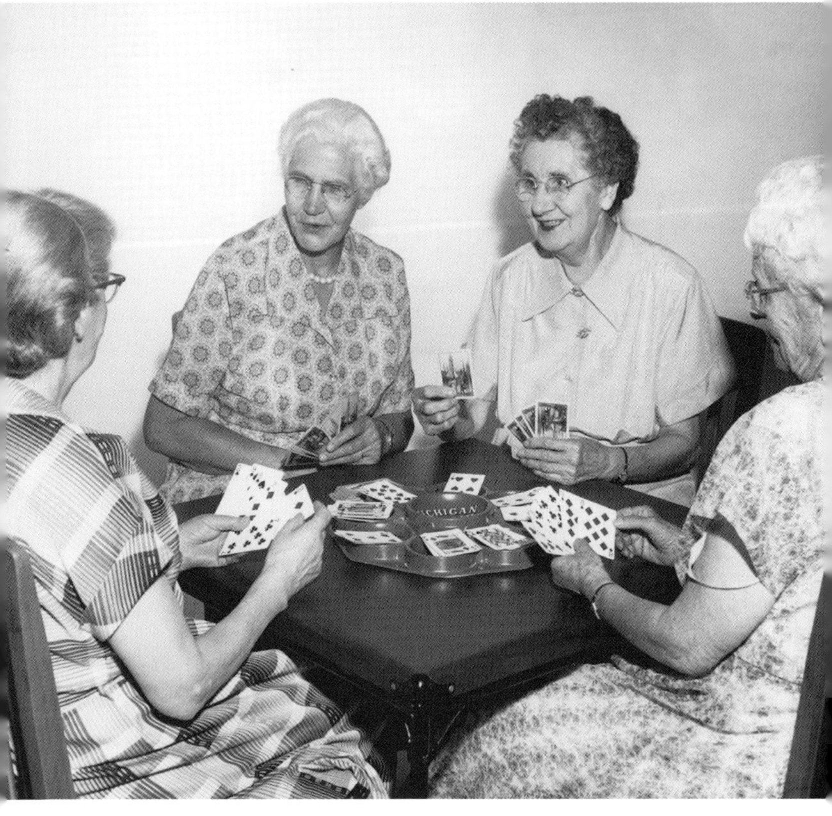
ICHIGAN

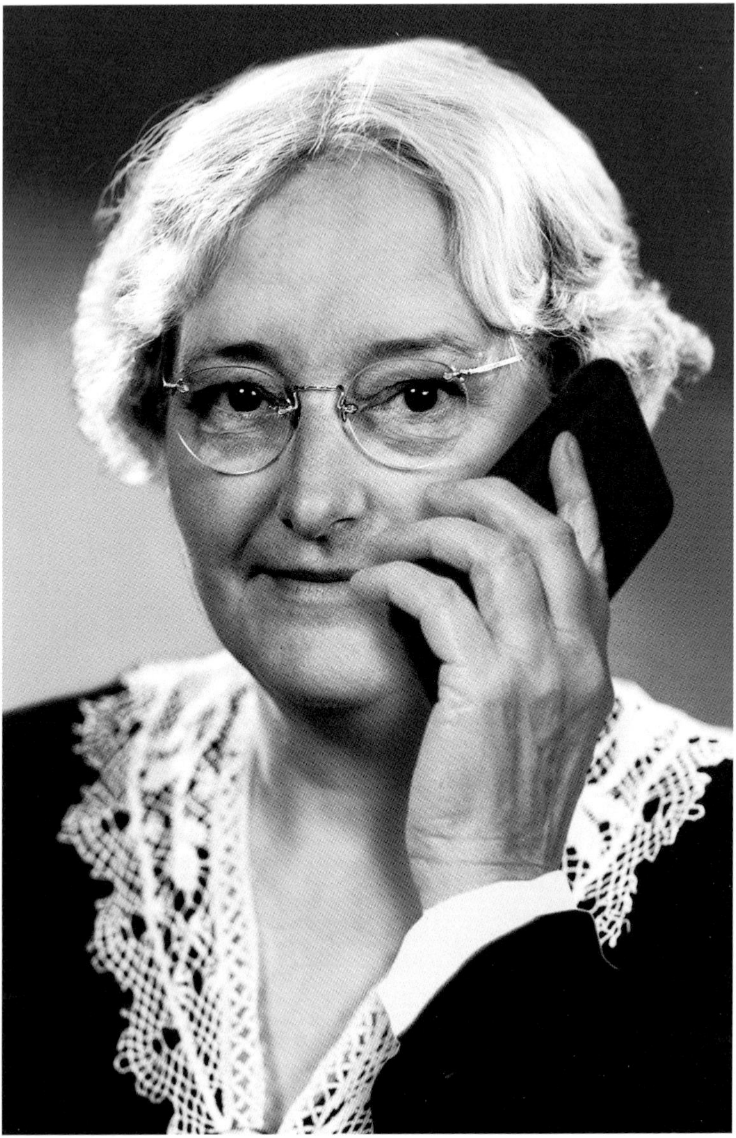

Grandma hadn't yet managed to make a call on her new smartphone, but she had got 17 photos of her left ear!

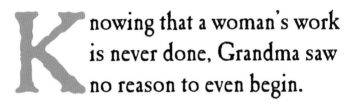

Knowing that a woman's work is never done, Grandma saw no reason to even begin.

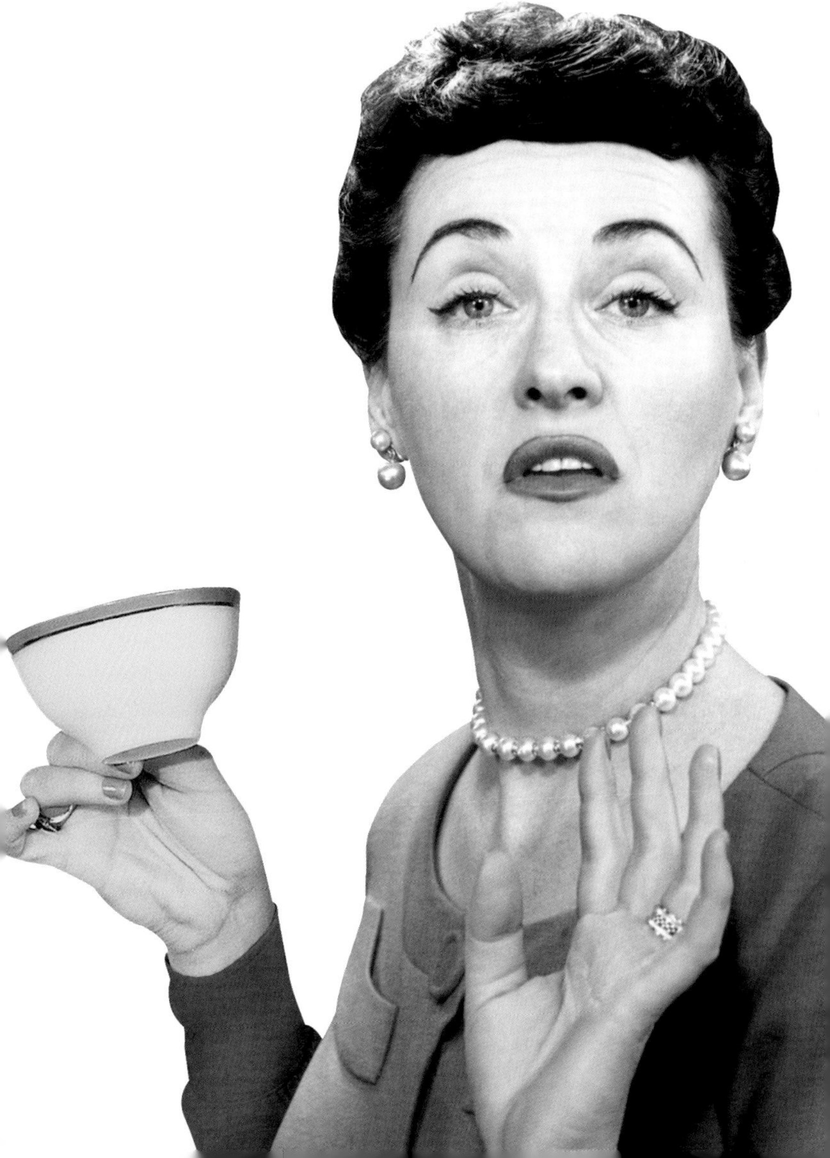

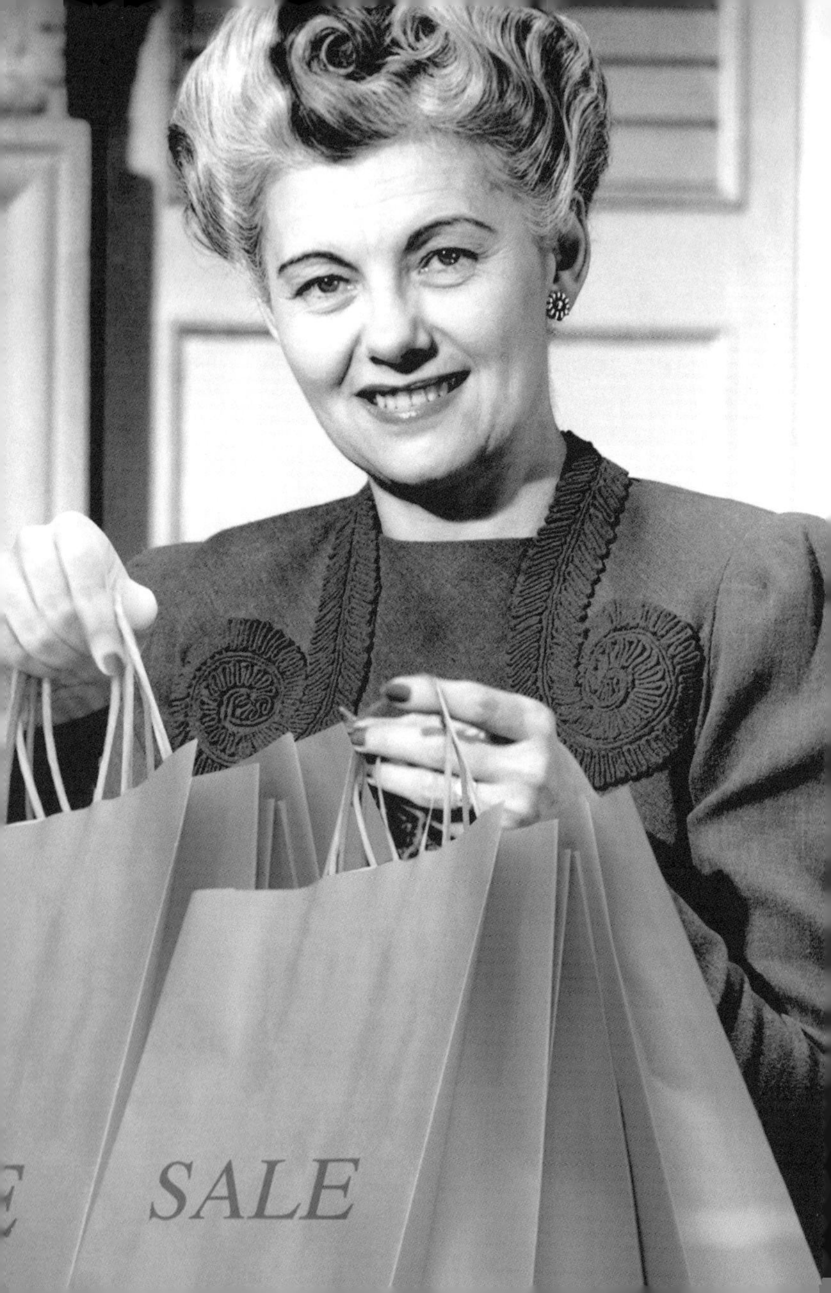
SALE

ithout her glasses
Grandma was always
walking into things.

Shops, mostly.

"Yeah, yeah, I'm the best Grandma in the world... blah, blah, blah... you told me this stuff last year. Where's my pressie?!"

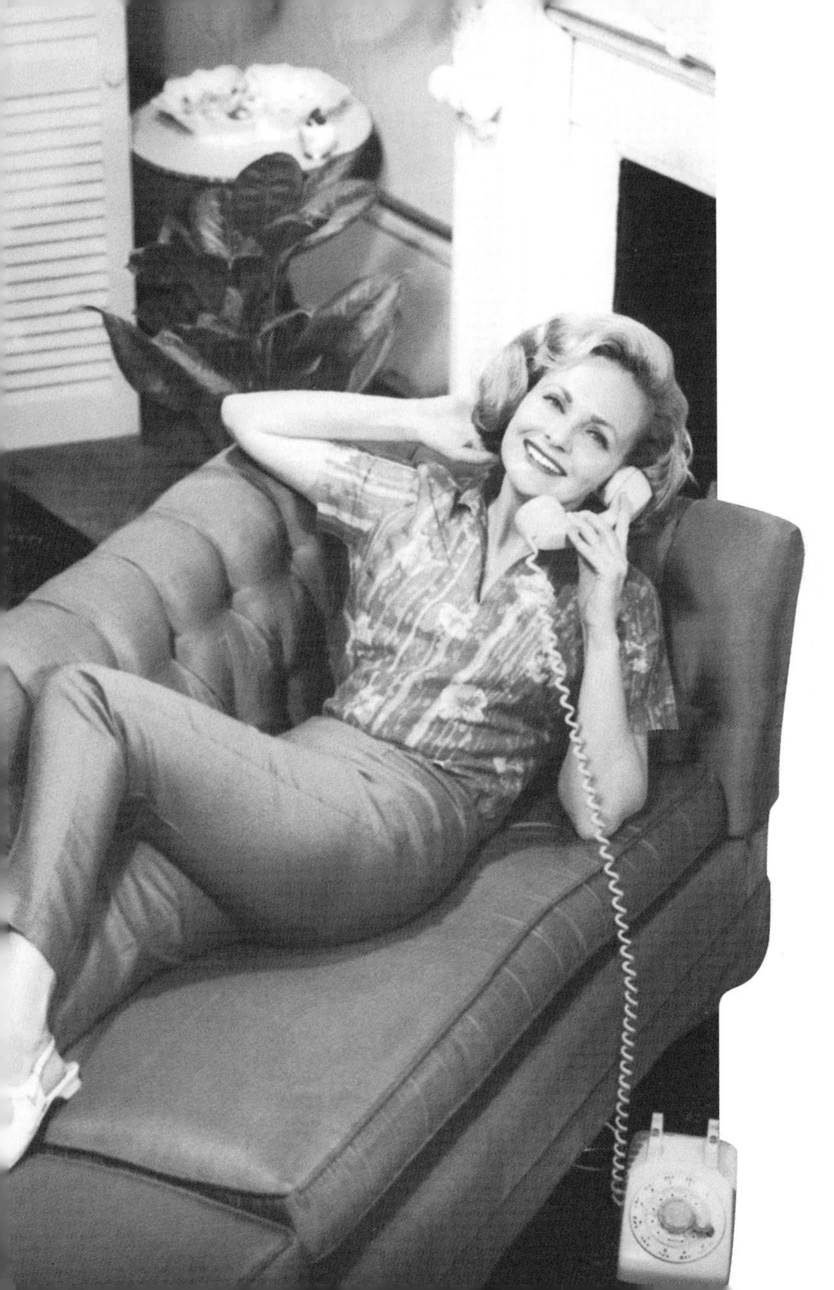

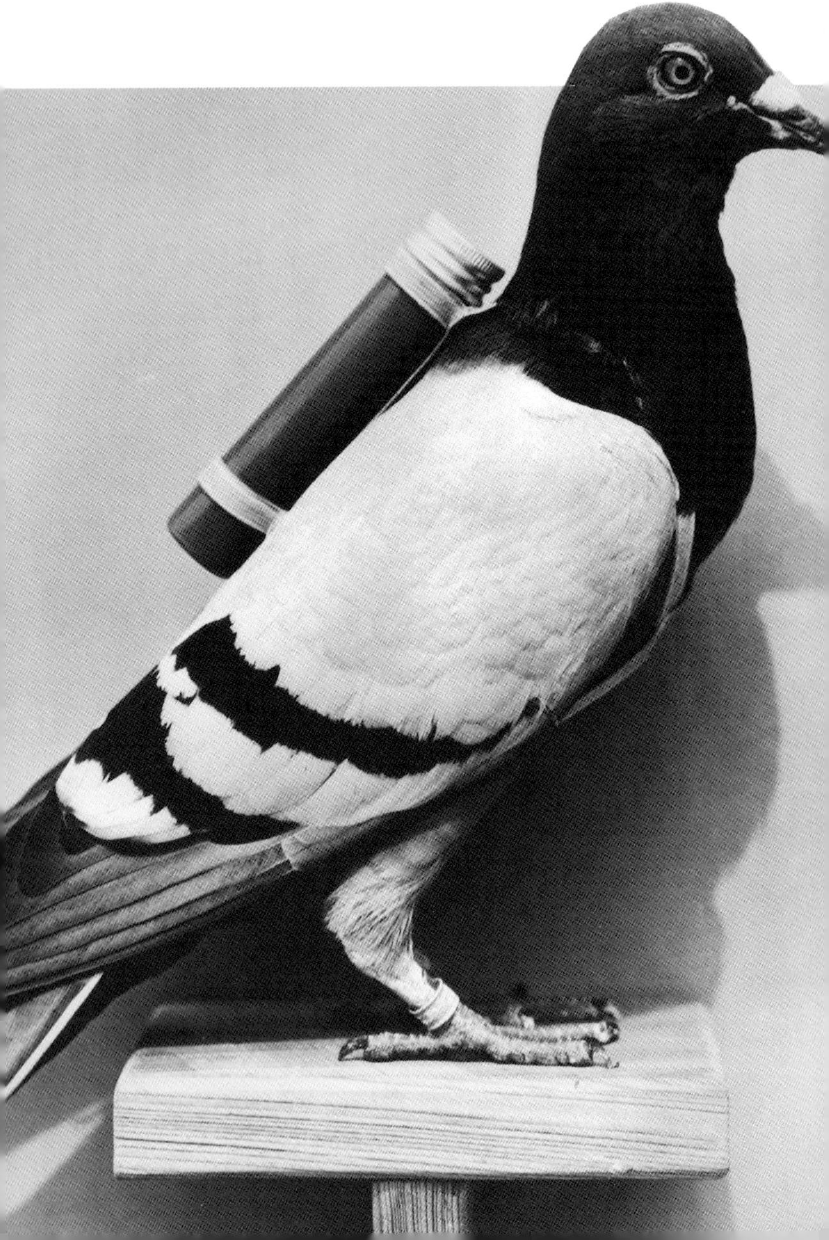

Eventually he decided that this would be much quicker than trying to teach Grandma how to use email.

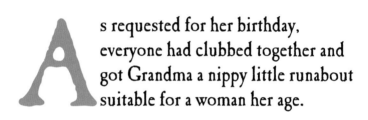

s requested for her birthday, everyone had clubbed together and got Grandma a nippy little runabout suitable for a woman her age.

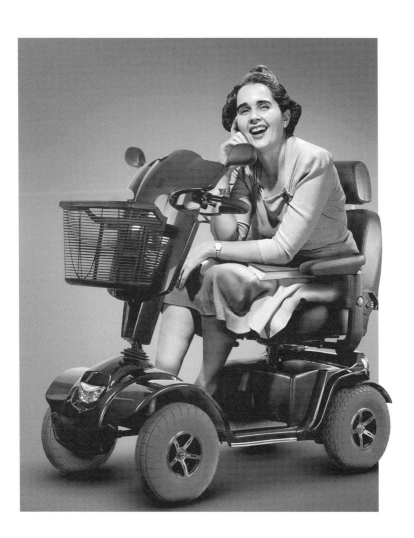

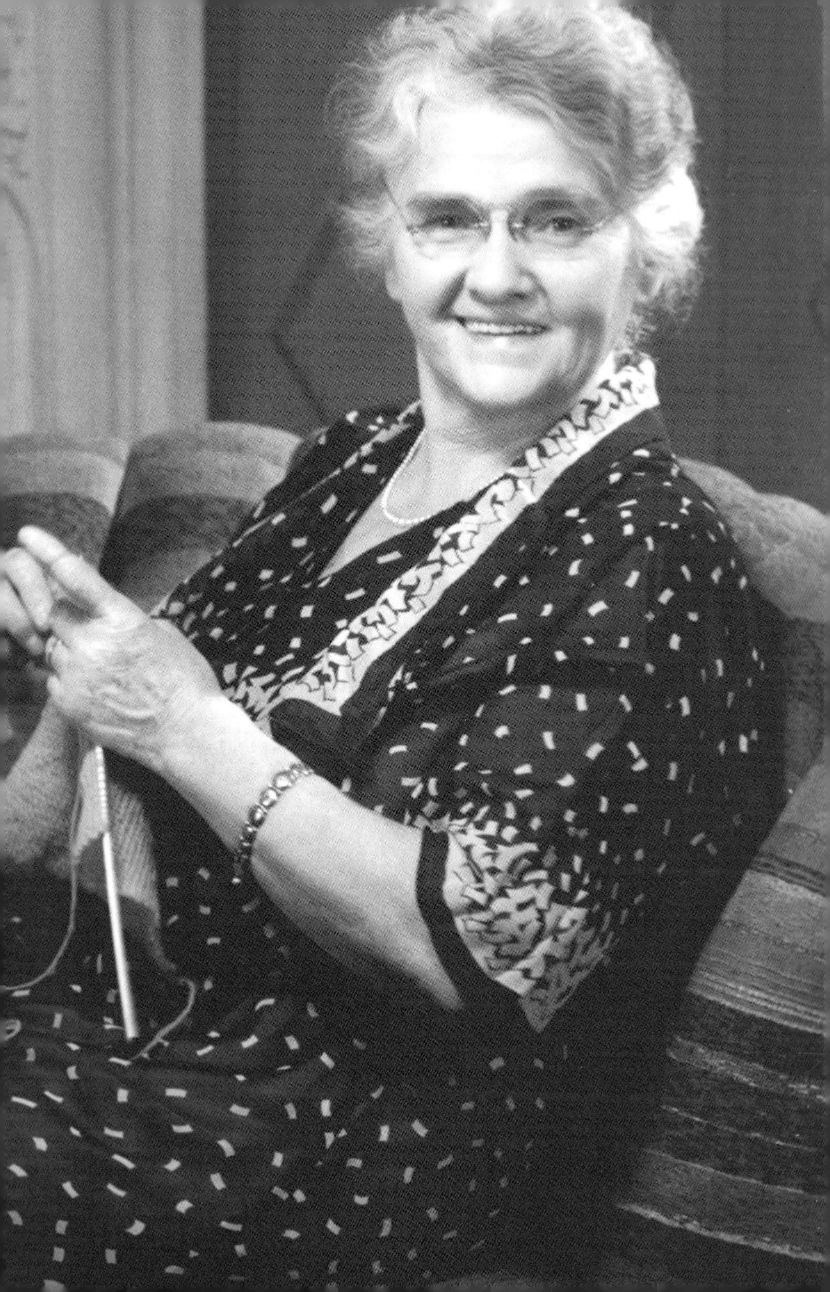

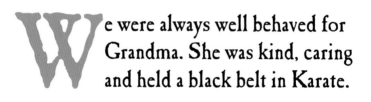

We were always well behaved for Grandma. She was kind, caring and held a black belt in Karate.

Grandma needed to drink...
... She had grandkids.

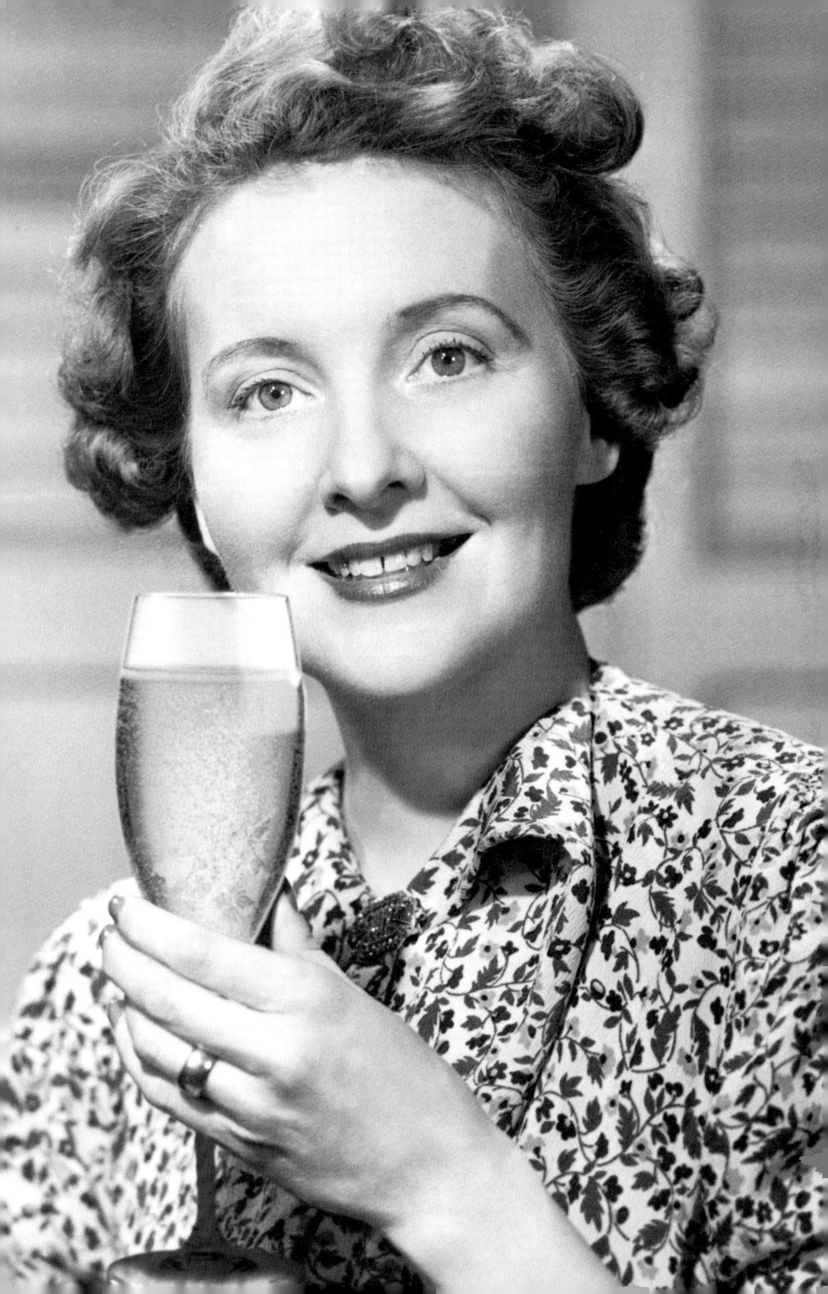

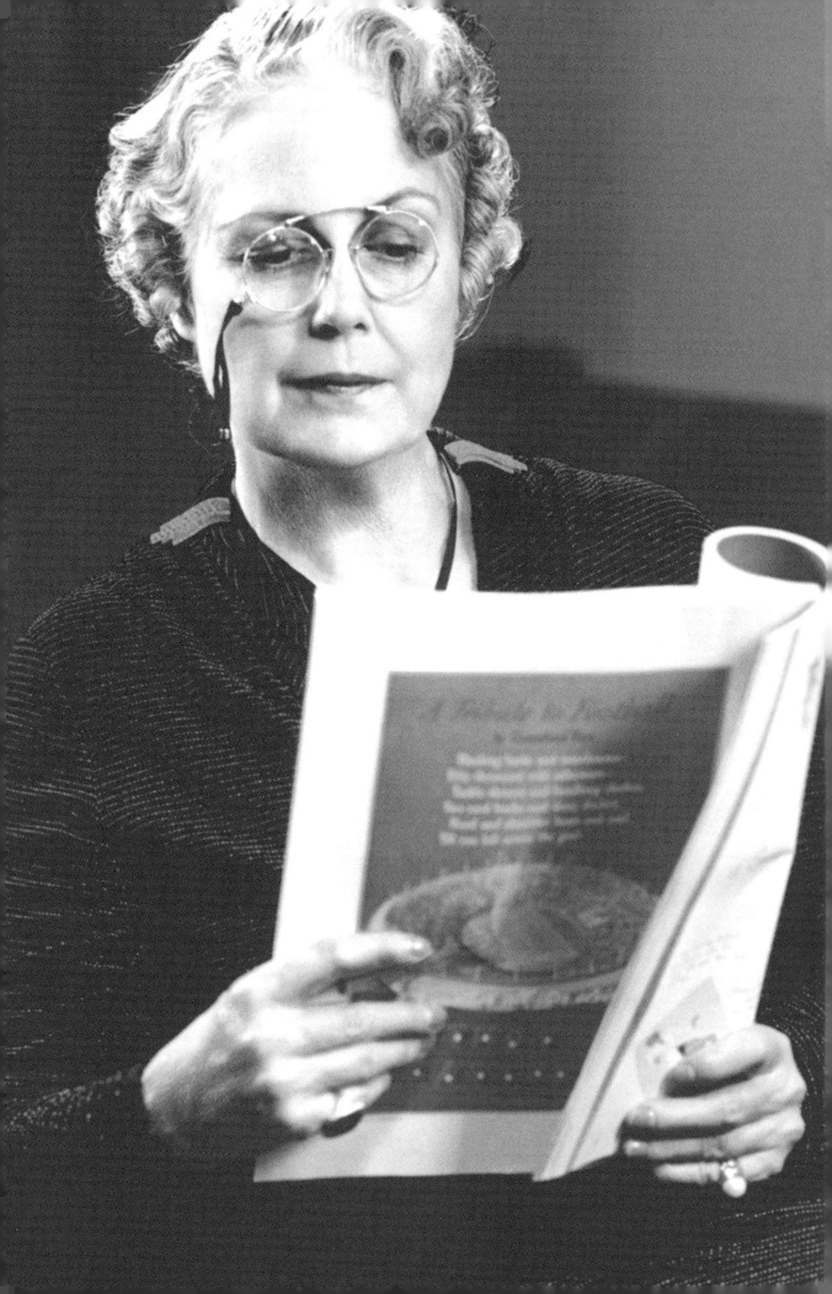

Having read so much about the ageing effects of both chocolate and alcohol, Grandma immediately decided to give up reading.

Finally, Grandma decided to clear out her handbag.

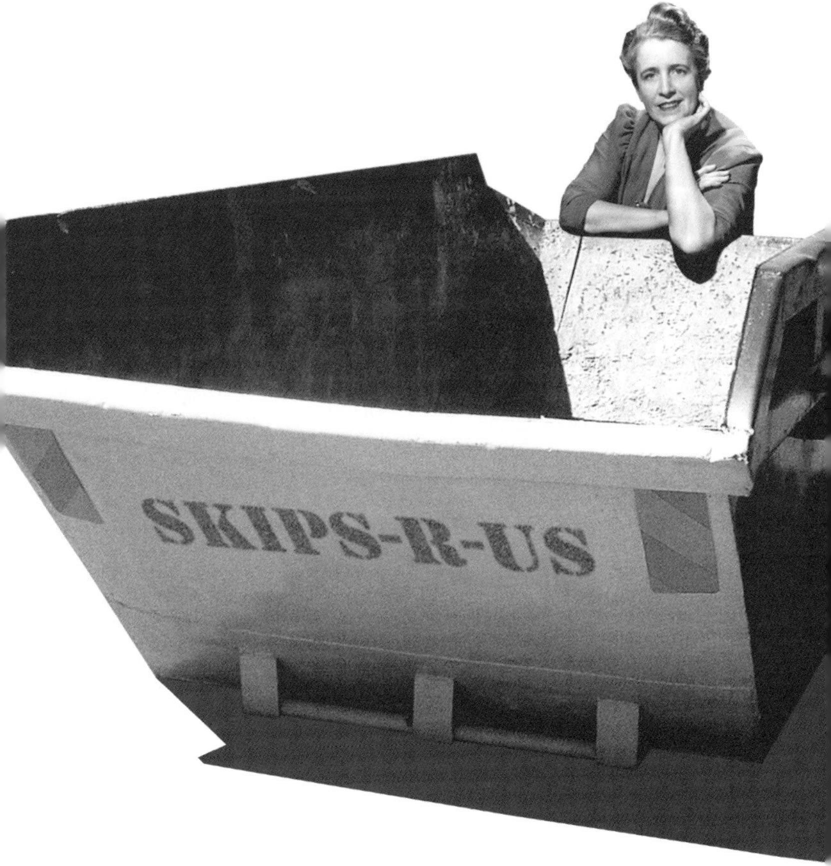
SKIPS-R-US

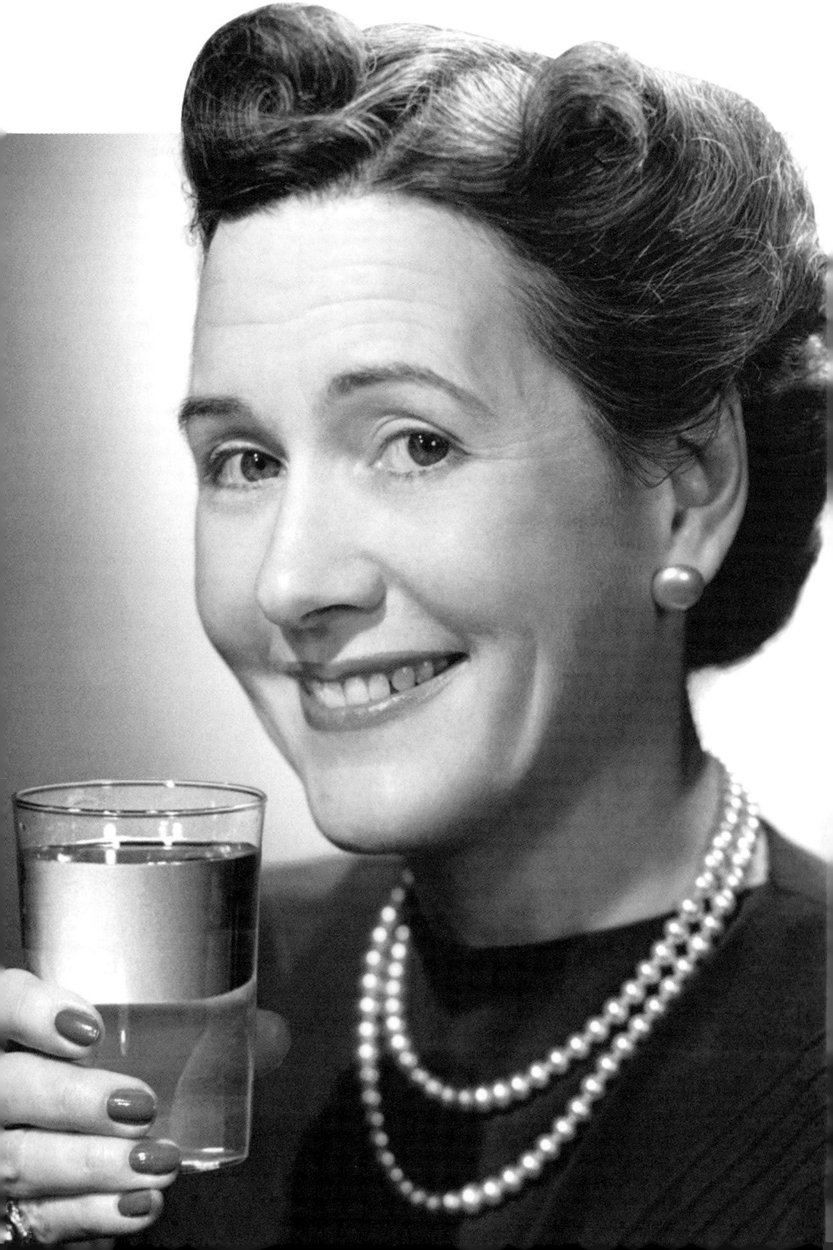

After trying to forget her age all day, Grandma decided, "If at first you don't succeed, try, try a gin!"

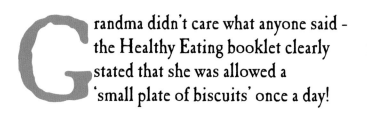

Grandma didn't care what anyone said - the Healthy Eating booklet clearly stated that she was allowed a 'small plate of biscuits' once a day!

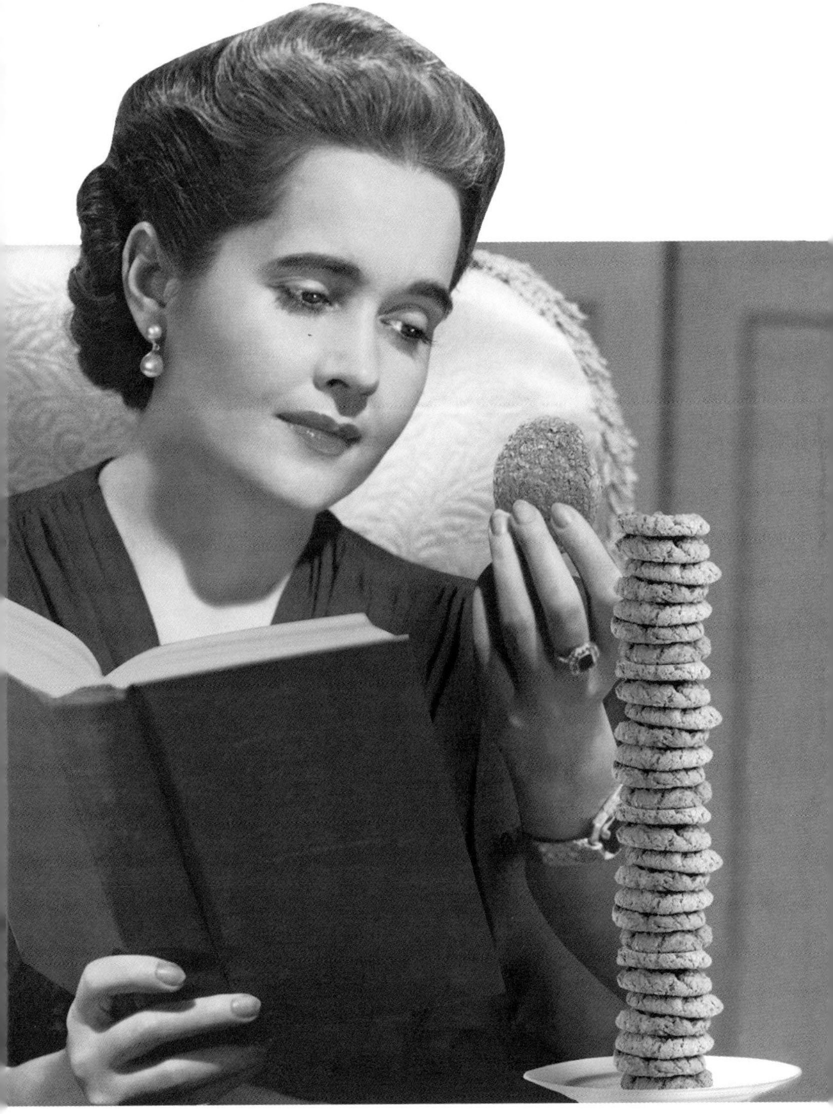

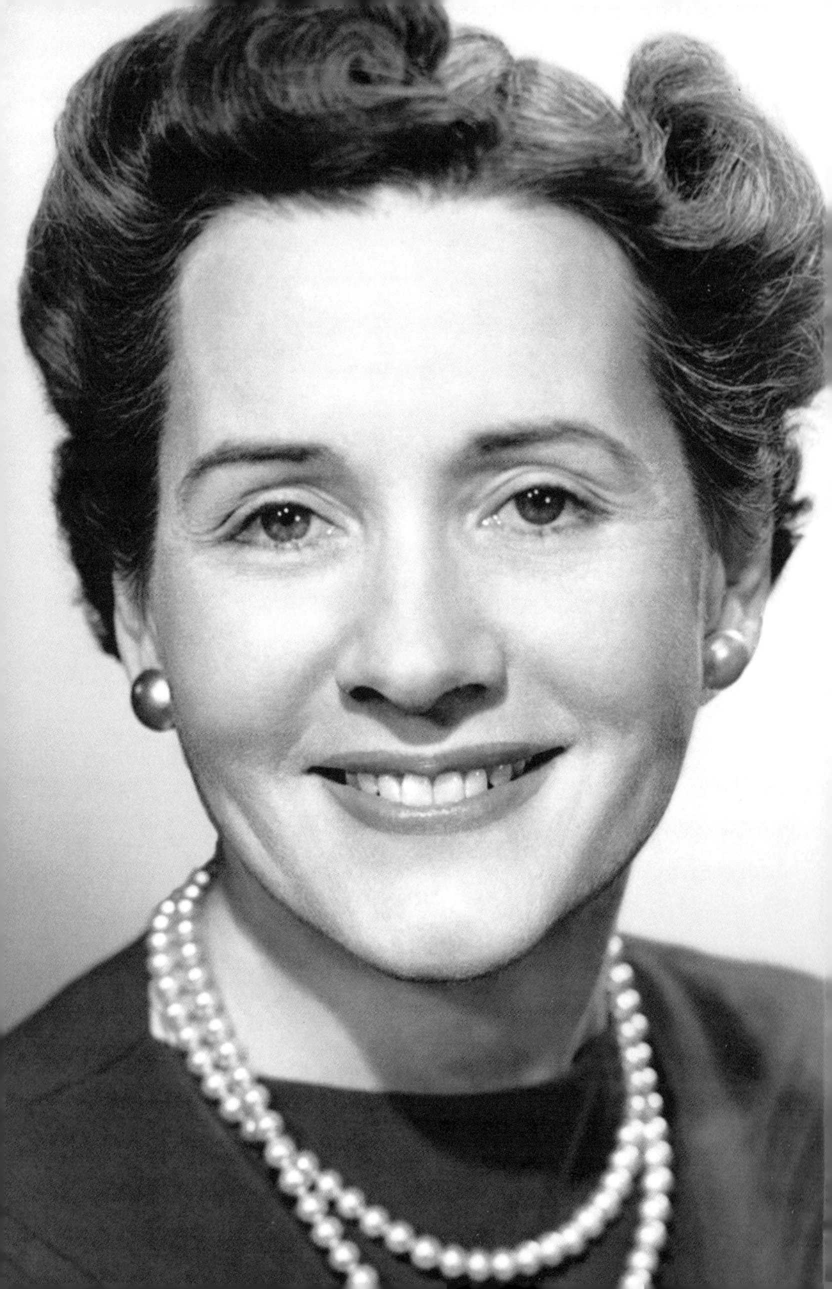

Of course Grandma wasn't old.
She was RETRO!

There was a dark moment in her life when Grandma caught a fleeting glimpse of a pair of elasticated trousers and secretly thought to herself 'Ooooh, they look comfy'.

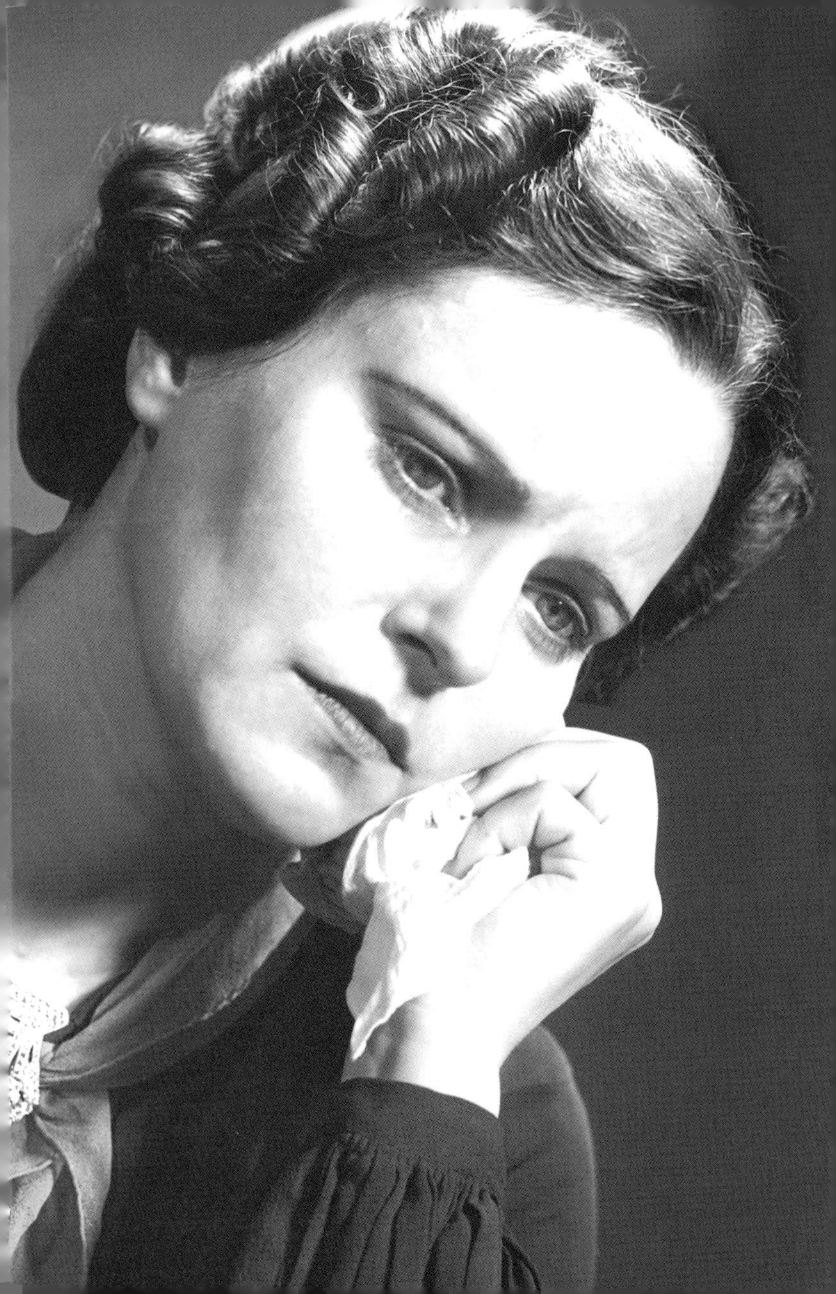

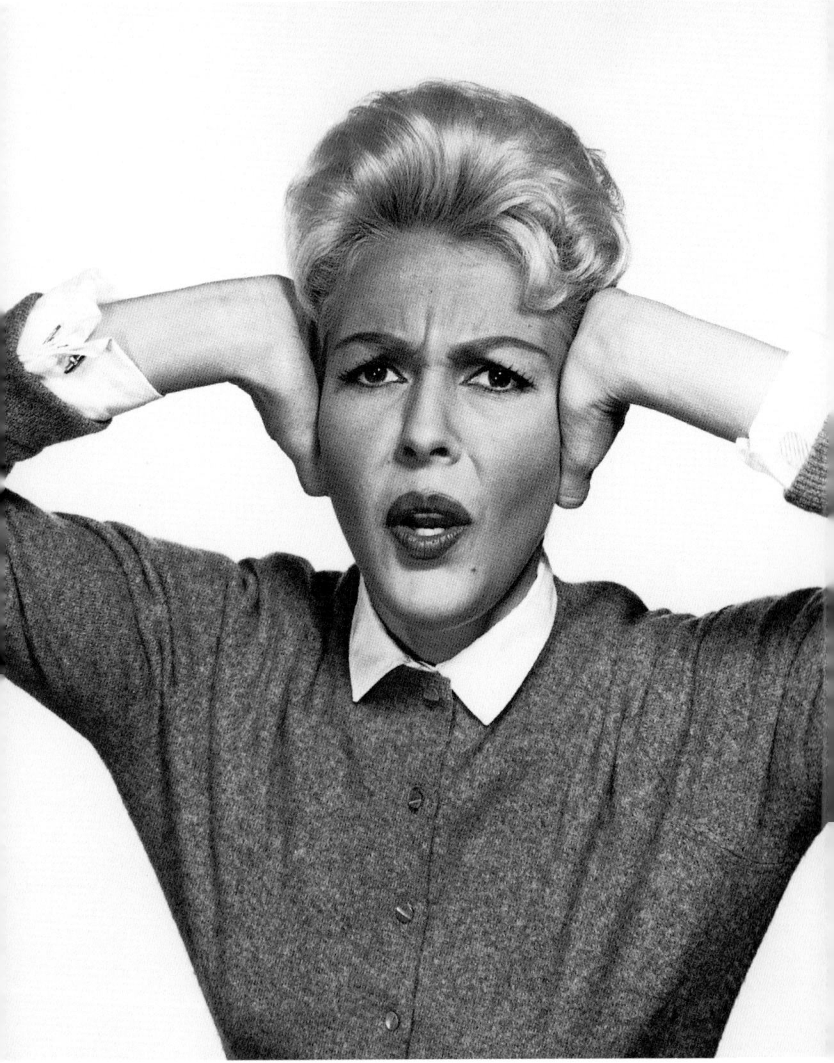

Grandma deduced from the frantic beeping of the smoke alarm that her grandchildren were trying to cook her breakfast.